THE SHARK

Silent Hunter

D1118551

3 1489 00551 0241

Renée Le Bloas-Julienne

Photos by the BIOS Agency

French series editor, Valérie Tracqui

ⅰ⌂ⅰ Charlesbridge

FREEPORT MEMORIAL LIBRARY

© 2007 by Charlesbridge Publishing. Translated by Elizabeth Uhlig.

© 2004 by Editions Milan under the title *Le Requin,* 2nd ed.
© 1997 by Editions Milan under the title *Le Requin,* 1st ed.
300 rue Léon-Joulin, 31101 Toulouse Cedex 9, France
www.editionsmilan.com
French series editor, Valérie Tracqui

All rights reserved, including the right of reproduction in whole
or in part in any form. Charlesbridge and colophon are registered
trademarks of Charlesbridge Publishing, Inc.

Published by Charlesbridge
85 Main Street
Watertown, MA 02472
(617) 926-0329
www.charlesbridge.com

Library of Congress Cataloging-in-Publication Data
Le Bloas-Julienne, Renée.
  [Requin, tueur silencieux. English]
  The shark, silent hunter / Renée Le Bloas-Julienne ; photos by
the Bios Agency ; [translated by Elizabeth Uhlig].
    p. cm. — (Animal close-ups)
    ISBN 978-1-57091-631-1 (softcover)
1. Sharks—Juvenile literature. I. Title. II. Series.
QL638.9.L3913 2007
597.3—dc22   2006009633

Printed in China
(sc) 10 9 8 7 6 5 4 3 2 1

PHOTO CREDITS
BIOS Agency: J.-C. Robert: cover, pp. 1, 6, 9, 16 (bottom), 20 (bottom left);
Y. Lefèvre: back cover, pp. 5, 6–7, 7 (bottom left), 8 (top), 10–11, 12–13, 14
(bottom left), 15 (top and bottom), 17, 25 (top right), 26 (middle); P. Fagot:
pp. 4–5; H. Ausloos: pg. 8 (bottom); J. L. Rotman: pp. 13 (middle), 20–21;
P. Kobeh: pp. 13 (top), 22; H. Caroll/P. Arnold: pg. 14 (right); K. Aitken/P.
Arnold: pp. 16 (top), 26 (bottom); J. L. Rotman/P. Arnold: pp. 19 (top), 21,
24 (top); Y. Tavernier: pg. 19 (bottom); R. Seitre: pg. 20 (bottom right);
F. Bavendam: pp. 22–23, 25 (top left), 27 (top and bottom); G. Martin: pg. 24
(bottom); D. Heuclin: pg. 26 (top).

PHONE Agency: E. Saunders/Auscape: pg. 25 (bottom)

P. Deynat: pg. 7 (bottom right); W. R. Strong: pp. 13 (bottom), 23; D. Doubilet:
pp. 18, 18–19.

SHARK IN SIGHT!

The enormous coral reef looks like a garden. Multicolored fish swim back and forth, searching for food along the reef. A moray eel peeks out from its hiding place.

Deeper down, crayfish walk in single file. Hungry crabs crack open shellfish with their claws. It's a noisy lagoon.

Suddenly a fin surfaces above the water. A dark form glides above the coral. It's a gray reef shark. It circles the reef in search of easy prey. Sensing a threat, the fish take cover as they watch the shark lurk about the reef. The hunter silently circles once more before disappearing into the deep blue.

Gray reef sharks can be found in warm, tropical waters. They live near coral reefs where there are plenty of fish and other prey.

Gray reef sharks usually swim in deep waters, but they come up to the surface when searching for prey.

A LIVE TORPEDO

Built for speed, gray reef sharks have torpedo-shaped bodies that glide easily and quietly through the water. They can accelerate with amazing speed, reaching up to twenty-five miles per hour. Their coloring helps them catch prey unawares. When seen from above, their dark gray backs blend in with the blackness of the deep waters. When seen from below, their white bellies are barely visible against the bright surface of the water. Gray reef sharks use their powerful tails to propel themselves forward, but they cannot swim backward. Two pectoral fins keep the sharks' bodies steady. Wide flippers allow the sharks to turn quickly.

Gray reef sharks can measure up to 6½ feet long.

A suckerfish attaches itself to a gray reef shark. This little fish eats the parasites that infest the shark's body.

Although most fish have swimming bladders to help them float, sharks don't. Instead they rely on their large, oil-filled liver to help keep them from sinking. The oil is lighter than water, which increases the sharks' buoyancy. Unlike other fish, which have bones, sharks have skeletons made of cartilage. Cartilage makes sharks light and flexible.

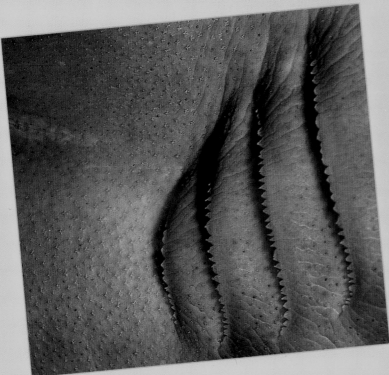

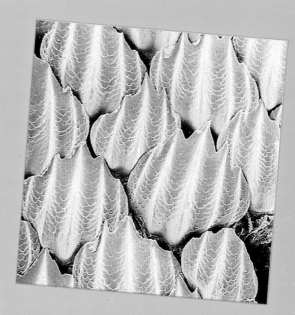

Denticles are grooved to allow water to pass smoothly over sharks' bodies.

Sharks don't have scales. Their skin is covered with thousands of teethlike projections called denticles.

SHARK TERRITORY

Gray reef sharks protect their territories. If a smaller shark species enters a gray reef shark's territory, there's trouble. Gray reef sharks do have to watch out for larger shark species, such as tiger sharks. Tiger sharks are aggressive predators and are one of the most dangerous shark species in the world. Although they live in the open sea, tiger sharks come to reefs in search of food. A tiger shark will attack a gray reef shark if it gets in its way.

The tiger shark is one of the most aggressive sharks in the tropical seas. They have been known to attack sea birds, other sharks, and even people.

Gray reef sharks attack when they are chased or frightened. First they give a warning by facing their enemy with their mouth partially open, their fins lowered, and their back arched.

When facing a tiger shark, the gray reef shark takes a defensive posture to intimidate its enemy. It moves around the tiger shark, sharply swaying its head and tail. It arches its back, lifts its snout, and lowers its fins into a "hunch" display.

If the intruder persists, then the gray reef shark attacks at the risk of being eaten. If the tiger shark decides not to fight, the sharks go their separate ways.

Gray reef sharks will seek out a new territory if there is not a plentiful food supply. Although they can be found in waters as deep as 3,000 feet, gray reef sharks are often seen along the outer reaches of reefs.

THE GATHERING

Coral reefs are alive with activity. Schools of fish search for food. Gray reef sharks that are in the area pick up the movements and noises that these fish make. All sharks have tiny receptors, called lateral lines, along both sides of their bodies. With these lateral lines, sharks can sense noise and movement. Once alerted to the presence of the fish, the sharks become excited.

Gray reef sharks from the surrounding area form a group. One, two, three, then ten, thirty—they arrive from all over, ready to hunt. Nervously, the sharks swarm. Gray reef sharks become aggressive when they sense that food is nearby. Although there is no single leader, smaller sharks defer to the larger members of the group. The sharks advance toward their prey with their snouts pointed forward. The hunt has begun.

During the day, gray reef sharks hunt in groups. There can be as many as 50 of them waiting in ambush.

ON THE HUNT

The gray reef sharks search for the school of fish. All their senses are alert. Using their lateral lines, the sharks pick up the movement of the school along the reef. If a fish is wounded or loses a few drops of blood, the scent is quickly detected. The hunters' heads sway and tilt as they follow the trail to the source of this appetizing smell.

When the sharks finally reach the school of fish, they use their excellent eyesight to choose their prey. As they near a fish, they use pores on the end of their snout to detect electrical waves emitted by the fish. These pores are called the ampullae of Lorenzini, and all sharks have them. With these pores, sharks can find their prey under sand, at night, or when their eyes are rolled back and they cannot see. The pores are a shark's sixth sense.

Sharks and rays are the only fish to have ampullae of Lorenzini. They pick up the presence of prey by sensing its electrical waves.

Using their lateral lines, sharks can detect movements of the fish and other nearby objects.

Here, the pores that make up a shark's ampullae of Lorenzini are visible on its snout.

A super sense of smell

Sharks use their gills to get oxygen. Sharks' nostrils are not designed for breathing; instead they are used to detect scents. Sharks have a sense of smell so sharp that they can pick up the scent of one drop of blood dissolved in 25 gallons of water. Water enters the shark's nostrils, and receptors process odors found in the water, letting the shark know if there is food nearby.

SHARK TEETH

Gray reef sharks are curious. They circle their prey many times to get a closer look. As the circles get smaller and smaller, the prey becomes terrified. Sometimes a shark will bump its prey with its snout to determine if it's worth eating.

When a gray reef shark is ready to attack, its eyes roll back in its head. The shark tips back its snout and opens its mouth wide. Its teeth, sharp as razors, bite down on the fish. The fish has been caught.

The shape of shark teeth varies. Gray reef sharks have triangular teeth.

Sharks have several rows of sharp teeth to help hold onto prey.

Sharks often go for days without eating, but they gorge themselves once they find food. This school of common jacks promises to be a feast!

Gray reef sharks prey on a number of fish, including common jacks, suckerfish, and snapper. They also eat squid, octopus, crayfish, and crabs. Sharks hunt both day and night; they need lots of food to maintain energy.

Sometimes during an attack, a shark loses a few teeth, but these are quickly replaced by a tooth from another row. When one tooth breaks off, another moves forward to take its place.

Some shark species dig around in reefs. Using their ampullae of Lorenzini, they easily track down hidden prey.

DANCE OF DEATH

The scent of blood will sometimes attract a group of gray reef sharks to a large, newly killed fish. The sharks become even more aggressive. The abundance of food, the excitement of the hunt, and the scent of blood send them into a frenzy. They suddenly can't control the urge to bite.

At feeding time the largest sharks eat first.

Once the feast is over, a shark becomes calm again.

It all happens quickly. The sharks twist, rip, and shake the fish with a fury. Bones crack between their teeth. Swimming round and round in a furious circle, the sharks spin in a swirling mass of flesh and blood. It is a terrifying scene. Finally the last mouthful is swallowed. Then, as if nothing had happened, the sea is calm. The sharks swim away peacefully.

Gripped with excitement, the sharks fight over the prey. Although the sharks appear out of control, if they bite each other it is purely by accident. They only want the food and don't intend to kill other sharks in the group.

MATING AND BIRTH

Sharks usually mature in their teens. At this time they will find a mate. After mating occurs, it takes about a year before the pups are born. Gray reef sharks are viviparous, meaning the pups are nourished in the womb and are born live. Not all sharks are viviparous. Some species lay eggs.

The female gray reef shark doesn't care for her pups after they are born. After giving birth, a hormone is released in the mother's body that causes her to lose her appetite. This prevents her from biting her pups. After they're born, the litter of one to six pups is left on its own. They stick together and look for small prey such as shrimp and small fish.

If they avoid capture and hunters, they will live on the reef for twenty-five years or more. In time, these silent prowlers will be the masters of the sea.

Gray reef sharks are viviparous. They give birth to small, live sharks.

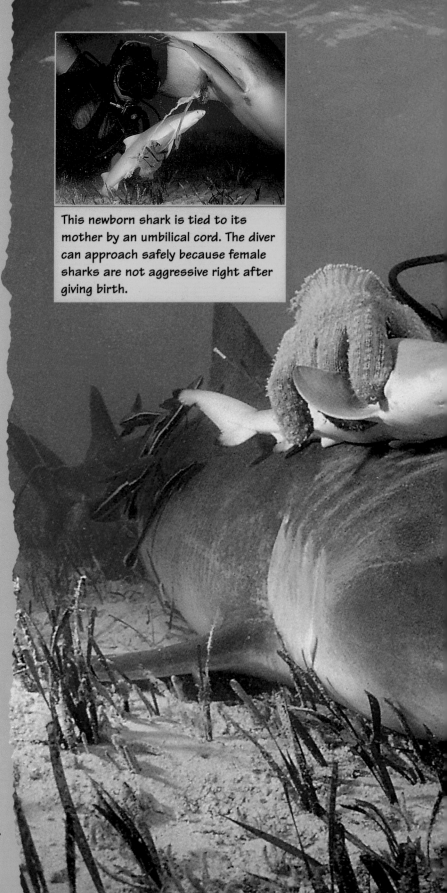

This newborn shark is tied to its mother by an umbilical cord. The diver can approach safely because female sharks are not aggressive right after giving birth.

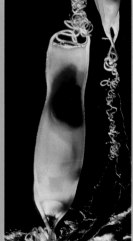

With ovoviviparous sharks, eggs are hatched inside the mother's body. The embryo (seen here) is nourished by a yolk sac.

Oviparous sharks lay eggs in a protective case, which they leave in the water to hatch.

FACE-TO-FACE

As a diver marvels at the beauty of the coral reef, she may be unaware that she's trespassing on the territory of a gray reef shark. When the shark senses the diver, it will draw near— not to eat her, but just out of curiosity. A shark's hunting instinct usually attracts it to more familiar prey. If a shark thinks that the human is a threat, though, it could attack.

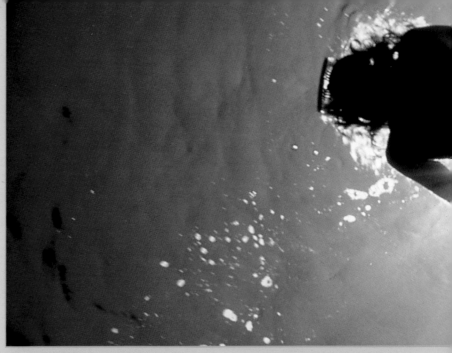

Sharks sometimes mistake humans for prey. So divers should always be aware of their surroundings.

To observe sharks, it is best to stay still with your arms kept close to the body.

Fin in sight!

Sharks attack people for a couple of reasons; they may be defending their territory or are overexcited by too much blood or movement. Sharks have different attack methods: hit-and-run, bump-and-bite, and sneak attack. In a hit-and-run, a shark bites its prey then leaves. Bump-and-bite is when a shark bumps its prey, bites it, then continues biting it. Attacking from below is a sneak attack.

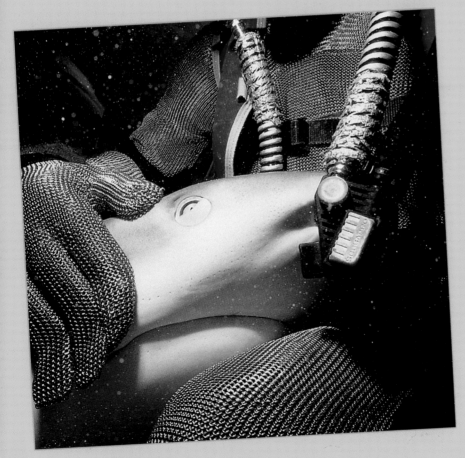

Some sharks have a membrane they can raise to protect their eyes.

Sharks tend to keep their distance while they are sizing up a diver. Many swimmers don't even notice a shark until it circles closer. If a shark approaches you, it's important not to panic and to just stay still. Movement will attract the shark. Don't take your eyes off the shark; sharks usually swim away from people who look directly at them. If the animal becomes too curious, play it safe and return to your boat or to the shore. A shark encounter is rare, but unforgettable.

EXTINCTION

Many people think that sharks are bloodthirsty and terrifying, but others are fascinated by these fierce creatures. These magnificent sea predators are neither good nor evil. They are simply deadly hunters. Unfortunately, sharks are in danger of becoming extinct because of commercial fishing and water pollution. Their future is still uncertain.

A TERRIBLE REPUTATION

In some countries shark fins are used for food. As demand for the fins grows, so does the threat to the shark's survival.

Sharks scare people, but most sharks have no interest in humans. Three shark species do present a real danger to humans: the great white shark, the bull shark, and the tiger shark. These sharks swim close to shore and will take a bite out of almost anything. Even so, shark attacks are rare. Unfortunately, humans kill millions of sharks each year.

FISHING OR MURDER?

Everything about the shark is useful, including its flesh, its liver oil, its blood, the cornea of its eyes, and its cartilage. But this feared creature is casually hunted and killed by humans. Thousands of sharks are thrown back into the water after their fins are cut off. This is a waste of a precious source of food and medicine and adds to the threat of extinction.

Many people think that the only good shark is a dead one. But sharks play an important role in the ocean's ecosystem. At the top of the food chain, they regulate life in the oceans and feed on animals that are weak, wounded, or sick. The disappearance of sharks would jeopardize the ocean's fragile balance. We are destroying them faster than they can reproduce, and several species are on their way to extinction. The shark's survival depends upon respect and tolerance by humans.

Fishnets can be fatal to sharks. The sharks get tangled up and cannot escape.

A passion for sharks

For the last 20 years, researchers have studied the life of these fierce predators. To do this, scientists mimic the sounds of fish, using underwater microphones and amplifiers. This immediately attracts sharks to the divers who are studying them. If the sharks attack, the scientists gently push them away by tapping their snout with a stick. The sharks will quickly turn away.

Scientists have found that most sharks are timid and will not attack humans unless they feel threatened. Sharks are great divers; some species can reach depths of 6,000 feet. Scientists are still learning about the habits and life of these amazing creatures.

OTHER SHARK SPECIES

Sharks belong to the class Chondrichthyes, along with rays, skates, and chimaeras. There are around 470 species of sharks in the world. All sharks have a skeleton made of cartilage and skin covered with denticles.

GREAT WHITE SHARK

Measuring up to 20 feet long and weighing over 4,000 pounds, great whites are massive sharks. Great whites have a worldwide presence and can be found in both warm and cold waters. They feed on fish, turtles, and dolphins.

BLACKTIP REEF SHARK

Blacktip reef sharks are well known in island waters and lagoons near the Indian and Pacific Oceans. They are able to swim in very shallow water and are often seen near the shore. They eat fish and squid.

WOBBEGONG SHARK

Wobbegongs are masters of camouflage. These carpet sharks, so named for their markings, are easily mistaken for the rocky ocean floor. They live in shallow, tropical waters in the Pacific and Indian Oceans, where they feed on octopus, crabs, and fish.

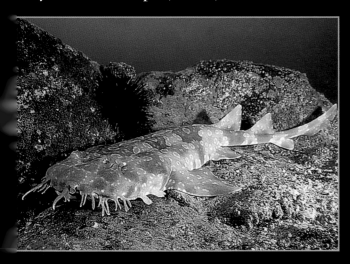

HAMMERHEAD SHARKS

Hammerheads have a unique-looking head that allows them to change direction quickly. They live in the warm waters of the Atlantic, Indian, and Pacific Oceans. They chase after agile prey, such as squid.

SAW SHARK

Saw sharks have long, flat snouts that are lined with teeth. They use their snout to knock down and shred prey, such as fish, shrimp, and squid. They live in ocean waters along Africa, Australia, and Japan. Saw sharks can be found at depths as great as 3,000 feet.

DOGFISH

Dogfish are small sharks, only about 2 feet long. They are often found on eastern Atlantic coastlines from Europe to Africa. They stay close to the ocean floor, feeding on mollusks and crustaceans.

OCEANIC WHITETIP SHARK

Oceanic whitetip sharks are migratory, covering great distances in one day. They are almost never found in shallow water; instead they spend their lives in deep ocean waters worldwide. They eat almost anything, including fish, turtles, and sea birds.

GRAY NURSE SHARK

Gray nurse sharks look terrifying, but this species is usually harmless. They spend most of their time close to the ocean bottom, searching for crabs and shrimp. They can be found in the Atlantic, Indian, and Pacific Oceans. They were almost hunted to extinction, but their numbers are increasing.

Whale shark

At almost 60 feet long and weighing 40 tons, whale sharks are the largest fish in the world. They feed on plankton and very small fish, such as mackerel and young tuna. These sharks live alone in tropical waters and are indifferent to humans.

Port Jackson shark

Port Jackson sharks are noted for the long spikes along their dorsal fins. They have large, flat teeth that crunch on sea urchins, crabs, starfish, and small fish. Port Jackson sharks can be found in Australia.

FOR FURTHER READING ON SHARKS . . .

Arnosky, Jim. *All About Sharks*. New York: Scholastic, 2003.

Simon, Seymour. *Sharks*. New York: Harper Collins, 1995.

Thomson, Sarah L. *Amazing Sharks!* (*I Can Read* Book 2). New York: Harper Collins, 2005.

USE THE INTERNET TO FIND OUT MORE ABOUT SHARKS . . .

NATURE: The Secret World of Sharks and Rays

—Offers general information on shark species, their behavior, and their natural history. Also includes reference links and sources for further reading.
http://www.pbs.org/wnet/nature/sharks/

Pelagic Shark Research Foundation

—Provides information on shark anatomy, conservation, and evolution. This site also discusses the shark species found at Monterey Bay Aquarium.
http://www.pelagic.org/

National Parks Conservation Association: Marine Parks: Sharks

—Filled with shark facts and trivia, this site describes the sharks found in the National Park System. Includes information on how to avoid a shark attack.
http://www.npca.org/marine_and_coastal/marine_wildlife/sharks.asp

INDEX